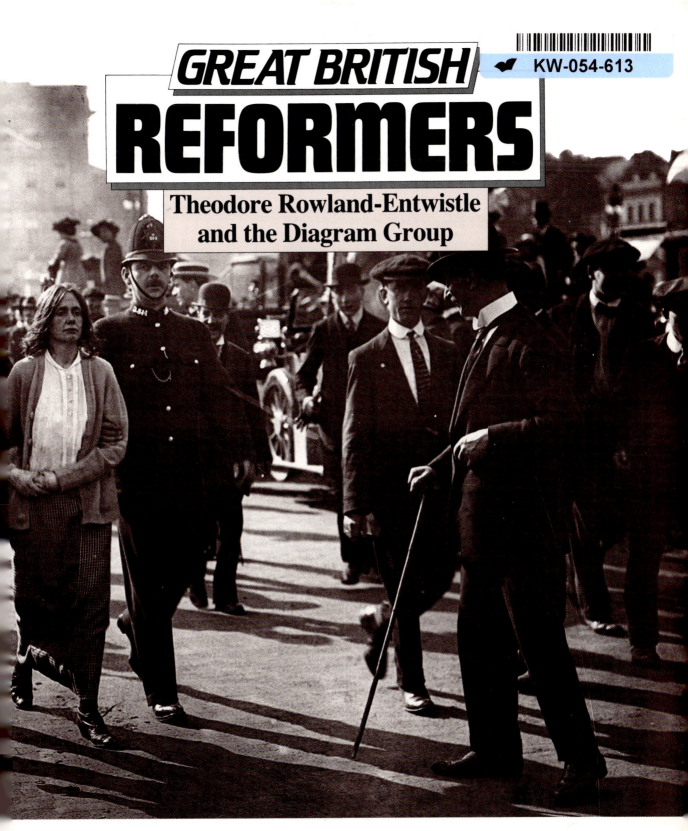

GREAT BRITISH
REFORMERS

Theodore Rowland-Entwistle and the Diagram Group

Franklin Watts
London New York Sydney Toronto

Members of the environmental group Friends of the Earth protesting to the Prime Minister about the pollution caused by the use of disposable cans and bottles

Acknowledgements
Picture research: IKON
Cover: Barnaby's Picture Library
Dr. Barnardo: 24
Derek Bayes: 35
BBC Hulton Picture Library: Inside cover–1, 12–13, 16, 17, 22, 23
The Guardian: 34
IKON: 15
The John Frost Newspapers Library: 32
Arthur Lockwood: 17
Mansell Collection: 8–9, 10–11, 19, 20, 23, 26, 29
The Museum of London: 29
National Portrait Gallery: 8, 18
Popperfoto: 31
The Salvation Army: 20, 21
Topham Picture Library: 2

KINGS AND QUEENS

ARCHITECTS

BOUDICA	EDWARD THE CONFESSOR	WILLIAM THE CONQUEROR	JONES	WREN	HAWKSMOOR
RICHARD I	EDWARD I	HENRY V		ADAM	NASH
HENRY VII	HENRY VIII		SOANE	SCOTT	SHAW
JAMES VI AND I	CHARLES I	CHARLES II	VOYSEY	MACKINTOSH	LUTYENS
GEORGE III	VICTORIA	ELIZABETH II	DREW	STIRLING	FOSTER

vitnbraus

A suffragette arrested outside Buckingham Palace

Contents

© Diagram Visual Information Ltd 1986

First published in Great Britain 1986 by
Franklin Watts Ltd
12a Golden Square
London W1

Printed in Singapore

ISBN 0 86313 366 5

When they lived

4

1756–1763 Seven Years' War in Europe

1815 Battle of Waterloo

1834 Abolition of slavery throughout British Empire

1854–1856 Crimean War

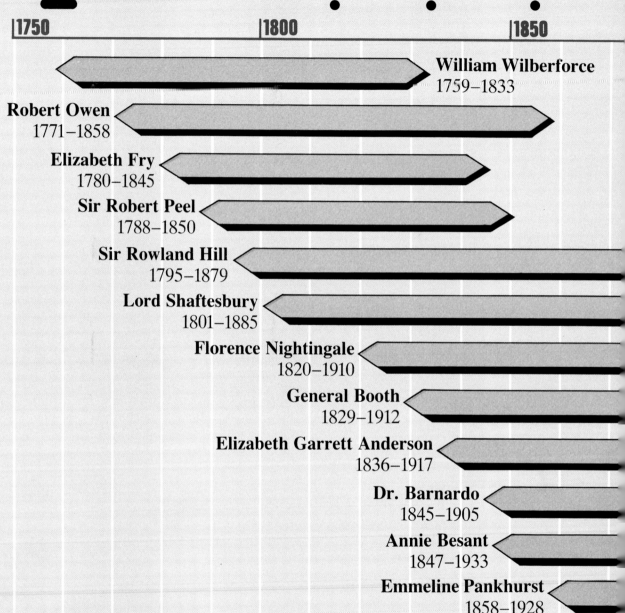

| 1750 | 1800 | 1850 |

William Wilberforce
1759–1833

Robert Owen
1771–1858

Elizabeth Fry
1780–1845

Sir Robert Peel
1788–1850

Sir Rowland Hill
1795–1879

Lord Shaftesbury
1801–1885

Florence Nightingale
1820–1910

General Booth
1829–1912

Elizabeth Garrett Anderson
1836–1917

Dr. Barnardo
1845–1905

Annie Besant
1847–1933

Emmeline Pankhurst
1858–1928

1750   1800   1850

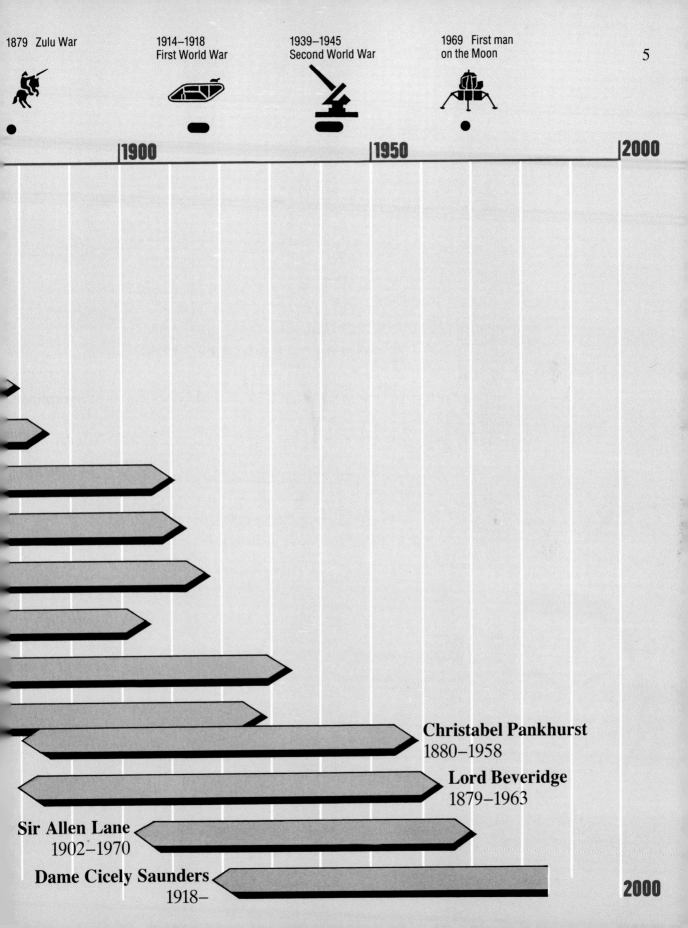

1879 Zulu War

1914–1918
First World War

1939–1945
Second World War

1969 First man
on the Moon

5

|1900 |1950 |2000

Christabel Pankhurst
1880–1958

Lord Beveridge
1879–1963

Sir Allen Lane
1902–1970

Dame Cicely Saunders
1918–

2000

William Wilberforce

William Wilberforce was one of the leaders of the campaign to abolish slavery. He was born in Hull in 1759, the son of a wealthy businessman. He went to Cambridge University, where he made a lifelong friend of William Pitt (later Prime Minister), and at the age of 21 was elected a Member of Parliament.

In London Wilberforce entered into society life, gambling and entertaining. Then he went on a tour of continental Europe, during which he was converted to active Christianity. Wilberforce changed his way of life. Since boyhood he had been interested in the slave trade, in which black Africans were taken to the Americas to work. At the age of 14 he had written to a newspaper denouncing the 'odious traffic in human flesh'. Now he resolved to fight against the trade.

In 1787 a group of abolitionists (opponents of the slave trade) asked Wilberforce to represent them in parliament. The abolitionists, who

TO BE SOLD & LET
BY PUBLIC AUCTION,
On *MONDAY the* 18th *of MAY,* 1829
UNDER THE TREES.
FOR SALE,
THE THREE FOLLOWING
SLAVES
VIZ.
HANNIBAL, about 30 Years old, an excellent House Servant, of Good Ch:
WILLIAM, about 35 Years old, a Labourer
NANCY, an excellent House Servant and Nurse

The MEN belonging to 'LEECHS' Estate, and the WOMAN to Mr D SMIT

A poster advertising the sale of slaves

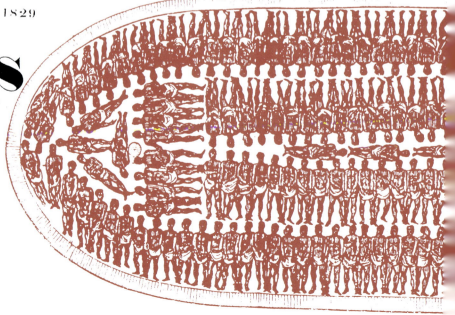

Overcrowding on board a slave ship (right)

included many Quakers, became known as the 'Clapham Sect' because they used to meet at the homes of some of their members in Clapham. Clapham, now part of inner London, was then a country village.

Wilberforce had a serious illness in 1788, and suffered from ill-health for the rest of his life. Time after time his attempts to push a bill through parliament to abolish the slave trade were voted down by the House of Lords, but in 1807 parliament finally agreed to ban the trade.

People in British colonies could still own slaves, and Wilberforce fought on to make this practice illegal, too. Illness forced him to retire from parliament in 1825. Eight years later, as he lay dying, he heard that his work was almost complete: a bill to abolish slave-owning was going through parliament. It became law just 30 days after he died.

1759
Born 24th August in Hull
1776
Went to Cambridge University
1780-1825
Member of Parliament
1785
Conversion to Christianity
1787
Began parliamentary fight against the slave trade
1794
Joined Society for the Abolition of the Slave Trade
1797
Published book entitled *Practical Christianity;* married Barbara Ann Spooner
1807
Slave trade abolished
1823
Founded Anti-Slavery Society
1833
Died 29th July in London; Slavery Abolition Act passed 28th August

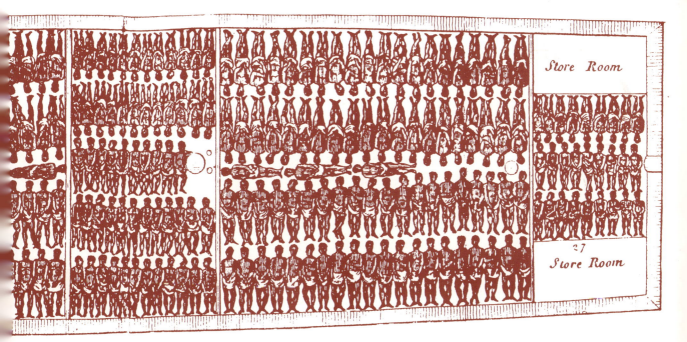

Robert Owen

The factories at New Lanark

Robert Owen was a pioneer of the Co-operative Movement, the forerunner of the Trade Union Movement, and an employer who cared for his workers. He was born in 1771 in Newtown, Powys, where his father was postmaster and an ironmonger. By the age of ten he was serving in a shop selling fabrics, and by the time he was 20 had become manager of a large Manchester cotton mill.

Owen's knowledge of fabrics and his skill at managing men brought him immediate success, and at the age of 24 he formed a partnership and set up a new cotton mill near Manchester. Later Owen and his partners bought the New Lanark Mills in Glasgow, and Owen married the daughter of their former owner.

At New Lanark Owen had 1,800 workers, including about 500 pauper children from the workhouses. He began putting his ideas for reform into operation. He improved the workers' slum

houses, opened a store where they could buy goods cheaply, and started Britain's first infants' school for their children.

Owen began writing about his views on social reform and education. His belief that people's characters are made by their circumstances won him support from political leaders in Britain, the United States, Austria, Prussia and Russia, and from the Duke of Kent, father of Queen Victoria.

Owen thought that people should live and work in communes, and set one up in New Harmony, Indiana, in the United States. This venture and others like it failed. He formed a trade union but it was suppressed by the government.

Owen lost popularity because he was against religion. As he grew older his views became more eccentric, he became a spiritualist, and he had little influence on his contemporaries. However, his pioneering work led to the development of the Co-operative Movement many years later.

The school room for the workers' children

1771
Born 14th May in Newtown, Powys
1781
Began work in a shop
1790
Became manager of large cotton mill in Manchester
1799
Married Anne Caroline Dale
1800
Took over New Lanark Mills
1816
Set up infants' school
1825
Founded commune in New Harmony, Indiana
1829
Retired from business
1833
Helped to found Grand National Consolidated Trades Union
1858
Died 17th November in Newtown

Elizabeth Fry

Elizabeth Fry visiting Newgate prison

1780
Born 21st May in Norwich
1800
Married Joseph Fry
1813
Began visits to Newgate
1817
Formed Association for the Improvement of the Female Prisoners in Newgate
1818
Visited jails in Scotland and northern England
1827
Visited Irish jails
1838-1843
Made tours of prisons in France, Belgium, Prussia, the Netherlands and Denmark
1845
Died 12th October in Ramsgate, Kent

Elizabeth Fry was one of the leaders of prison reform. She was born in Norwich in 1780, and was a member of a wealthy Quaker family, the Gurneys. At the age of 17 she resolved to dedicate her life to the service of God, and began visiting the poor. She started a school in the attic of the family home, teaching 60 poor children to read and write.

When she was 20 Elizabeth Gurney married Joseph Fry, who was a banker and also a Quaker. She continued her teaching and her religious work, at the same time bringing up a family of 11 children.

In 1813 she heard about the appalling conditions in Newgate, then the largest and most notorious of London's prisons. She went to see conditions for herself. She found men, women and children all herded together, hardened criminals rubbing shoulders with people awaiting trial for minor offences. In one filthy room there were 300

Elizabeth Fry reading to the women prisoners at Newgate

women, many of them drunk, fighting and swearing. To the surprise of the jailers, Mrs Fry was welcomed by the prisoners, who listened to her with respect.

She visited Newgate regularly, and started a school for the children. She provided materials so that the women could make and mend their children's clothes. The authorities at first opposed her reforms, but she was able to show that prisoners behaved better when treated decently.

As a result of her work women warders were engaged to supervise women prisoners, accommodation was improved, and jails were inspected regularly.

Between 1818 and 1843 Mrs Fry visited prisons in northern England, Ireland, France, Belgium, the Netherlands, Prussia and Denmark, where her ideas for prison reform were warmly received. Ill-health at last forced her to give up her travels, and her last years were spent as an invalid.

Sir Robert Peel

Robert Peel reformed the criminal law and taxes on food, and founded police forces in Ireland and London. Peel was born in Bury, Lancashire, the son of a wealthy cotton manufacturer. After a brilliant academic career at Oxford University, he became a Tory Member of Parliament at the age of 21, and three years later was Chief Secretary for Ireland. To deal with the lawlessness prevailing in Ireland, Peel set up a national police force, the Royal Irish Constabulary - whose members became known as 'peelers' after their founder.

Back in England, Peel held the office of Home Secretary for nearly eight years. During this time Peel revised the antiquated criminal laws, reducing the number of crimes punishable by death from more than 200 to about 100. He also formed London's Metropolitan Police Force, whose officers were quickly dubbed 'bobbies' after him.

Peel supported a law allowing Roman Catholics

1788
Born 5th February in Bury
1809
First became an MP
1812-1818
Chief Secretary for Ireland
1814
Formed the Royal Irish Constabulary
1820
Married Julia Floyd
1822-1830
Home Secretary
1829
Formed the Metropolitan Police in London
1834-1835
Prime Minister for four months
1841-1846
Prime Minister again; cut all export duties and repealed the Corn Laws
1850
Died 2nd July in London

'Peelers' in Bow Street, London

to have the vote, sit in parliament, and hold public office. He feared that if the law were not passed there would be civil war in Ireland, where most of the population were Catholic.

In 1830 Peel succeeded to his father's title of baronet, and it was as Sir Robert Peel that for a few months in 1834-1835 he was Prime Minister. At this time he set out the principles which changed the old Tory Party into the Conservative Party. He was Prime Minister again from 1841 to 1846. In this period Peel drastically cut import duties on a wide range of products, and abolished export duties.

His greatest achievements were the foundation of the Metropolitan Police, the repeal of the Corn Laws (which had kept the price of bread artificially high) and the establishment of Free Trade. The repeal of the Corn Laws split the Conservatives, and Peel was forced to resign. Four years later he fell from his horse and was fatally injured.

Sir Robert Peel

Sir Rowland Hill

Official notice of penny postage *(right)*

POST OFFICE REGULATIONS.

On and after the 10th January, a Letter not exceeding **half an ounce in weight,** may be sent from any part of the United Kingdom, to any other part, for **One Penny,** if paid when posted, or for **Twopence** if paid when delivered.

THE SCALE OF RATES,

If paid when posted, is as follows, for all Letters, whether sent by the General or by any Local Post,

Not exceeding ½ Ounce ....**One Penny.**
Exceeding ½ Ounce, but not exceeding 1 Ounce..**Twopence.**
Ditto   1 Ounce................2 Ounces **Fourpence.**
Ditto   2 Ounces ....3 Ounces **Sixpence.**

and so on; an additional Two-pence for every additional Ounce. With but few exceptions, the WEIGHT is limited to Sixteen Ounces.

If not paid when posted, double the above Rates are charged on Inland Letters.

1795
Born 3rd December in Kidderminster
1819-1833
Taught in various schools
1827
Married Caroline Pearson; moved to London
1833
Retired from teaching
1837
Published *Post Office Reform*
1840
Penny post introduced
1846-1864
On staff of Post Office
1860
Awarded knighthood
1879
Died 27th August in London

In the early 1800s postage was expensive, and quite beyond the means of most poor people. The charge for letters was paid by the person receiving them, and was based on the distance they were carried. The world owes its modern system of prepaid postage and standard charges to a retired schoolmaster, Rowland Hill.

Hill was born in 1795 in Kidderminster, Worcestershire. He began teaching mathematics - for which he had a talent - in his father's school at the age of 12. Ill-health forced him to give up teaching in 1833.

Hill was always interested in social reform, and had introduced a system of self-discipline and student democracy into his school. His mathematical mind turned to reforming the postal system, which he felt was not only inefficient but was not making as much money as it should.

In 1837 Hill produced a pamphlet in which he

quoted figures to show that cheap postage would result in many more letters being sent, and therefore more money coming in. He recommended a universal postage rate of 1d (less than 1p) for ordinary letters, to be paid by the sender.

Payment, he suggested, might be recorded on 'a bit of paper just large enough to bear the stamp and covered at the back by a glutinous wash which by applying a little moisture might be attached to the back of the letter'. As a result the penny post was introduced in January, 1840, and the first adhesive postage stamps went on sale on 6th May, 1840.

Hill held various jobs at the Post Office, and was knighted in 1860. By the time he finally retired in 1864, with a handsome pension, the number of letters posted every year had risen from 77,000,000 to 642,000,000.

London's first post box

Early postage stamps

Lord Shaftesbury

Anthony Ashley Cooper, later the sixth Earl of Shaftesbury, was one of the greatest reformers of the 1800s, particularly remembered for the relief he brought to workers in factories and mines.

His father succeeded to the earldom in 1811, and Anthony was known by the courtesy title of Lord Ashley. He was elected to the House of Commons in 1826, and he remained an MP, with one short break, until he became earl in 1851.

A deeply religious person, Ashley was appalled at the conditions under which poor people worked and lived. His diary shows that he was a gloomy man, with a strong feeling of duty and no sense of humour.

The first act passed as a result of his efforts was the Coal Mines Act of 1842, which banned boys under 13 and all females from working down the mines. The same year a group of factory reformers asked him to represent their views in parliament. Meanwhile Ashley was campaigning to have lunatics treated as 'persons of unsound mind' rather than as social outcasts. This was accomplished in the Lunacy Act of 1845, although prejudice remained. In 1847 the Ten Hours Act limited the working hours of people in factories.

In 1848 Ashley became Chairman of the Board of Health, set up during a cholera epidemic. For 40 years he worked to help set up ragged schools - free schools for poor children. After a long fight he succeeded in having boys banned from climbing chimneys to sweep them.

Shaftesbury's name and work are commemorated by London's Shaftesbury Avenue and the statue of Eros in Piccadilly Circus, which really represents the Angel of Christian Charity.

Lord Shaftesbury exploring the London slums in 1840

1801
Born 28th April in London
1811
Received courtesy title of Lord Ashley
1822
Graduated from Oxford University
1826-1830
MP for Woodstock
1830
MP for Dorchester
Married Lady Emily Cowper
1831-1846
MP for Dorset
1832
Took up cause of factory reform
1834-1885
Chairman of the Lunacy Commission
1835-1835
Served as a Lord of the Admiralty
1842
Coal Mines Act
1845
Lunacy Act
1847
Ten Hours Act
1847-1851
MP for Bath
1851
Succeeded as seventh earl
1867
More Factory Acts passed
1872
Lady Shaftesbury died
1875
Chimney Sweeps Act
1885
Died 1st October in Folkestone

Illustration from the Report to parliament showing women and children working in the mines

Florence Nightingale

Nursing was not always the respected profession it is today. Little more than a century ago the sick were mostly cared for by women with no professional training. So when Florence Nightingale told her wealthy parents that she wanted to be a nurse, they were appalled. In spite of violent opposition from her mother and sister she contrived to get some training in Germany, and in 1853 she became head of a hospital for gentlewomen in London.

Next year reports came of the suffering of British troops fighting in the Crimean War in Russia. Lack of medical care was killing more soldiers than the fighting. Sidney Herbert, the Secretary for War, asked Miss Nightingale to go out to the base hospital at Scutari in Turkey with a band of female nurses. She found appalling conditions and immediately demanded such basic necessities as good drainage, hot water, clean linen and soap. She had to fight hostility from the

Casualties on the battlefield

army doctors, and regulations that gave nobody authority to take the drastic action needed. In spite of opposition she improved conditions so far that the death rate from disease fell from more than 50 per cent to just over 2 per cent. At night she went round the wards with a lantern, and the soldiers called her 'The Lady with the Lamp'.

Miss Nightingale returned to England with her health shattered. Though mostly confined to bed she worked long hours, writing a 1,000-page report on army health and leading the drive to reform army medical care. The public had raised £45,000 in honour of her work in the Crimea. She used it to open the first training school for nurses, at St Thomas' Hospital in London.

For more than 40 years she was consulted by statesmen and nurses on medical matters, until her sight and her memory failed. She was the first woman to be awarded the Order of Merit.

1820
Born 15th May in Florence, Italy
1851
Trained in Germany
1854
Sent to Scutari to nurse Crimean War soldiers
1856
Returned to England
1857
Became permanent invalid; wrote report on army health
1860
Founded nursing school at St Thomas' Hospital
1861-1865
Advised on hospital care in American Civil War
1901
Lost her sight
1907
Awarded Order of Merit
1910
Died 13th August in London

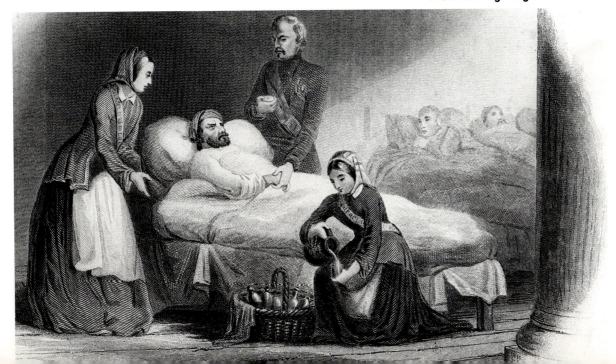

Florence Nightingale at Scutari

General Booth

The world's most peaceful army was the life work of William Booth, a preacher who made war on the dreadful conditions in which millions of poor people lived, conditions which drove many of them to drink.

Booth was born in Nottingham in 1829. His first work was as apprentice to a pawnbroker. At the age of 14 he became converted to Christianity, and began preaching. Five years later he moved to London, and there he was engaged by a group of Methodists as a lay preacher. He was ordained as a Methodist minister at the age of 29.

Meanwhile Booth had met and married Catherine Mumford, daughter of a Methodist carriage-builder. She was much better educated and was able to help Booth in many ways. In turn, he fired her with his zeal for saving souls. Although she was a semi-invalid all her life, she bore and brought up eight children, and spent a lot of her time preaching.

In 1861 Booth left the Methodists to devote all

1829
Born 10th April in Nottingham
1843
Worked for pawnbroker
1852
Became Methodist lay preacher; married Catherine Mumford
1858
Ordained as a minister
1861
Left the Methodists
1865
Started London mission
1878
Adopted name Salvation Army
1890
Catherine Booth died
1912
Died 20th August in London

Selling copies of *The War Cry* in public houses

his time to travelling up and down the country, preaching to large crowds and making many converts. Then Catherine persuaded him to start a mission in the East End of London. Booth ruled the mission strictly, and his colleagues called him 'The General'. He declared war on evil, and from this military language came the name the Salvation Army, which he adopted officially in 1878.

For many years Booth and his 'soldiers' were mocked, beaten up and even arrested. Gradually the value of their work was recognised. The Salvation Army's officers penetrated the worst slums, and persuaded drunkards to reform their ways. They founded hospitals and homes for the destitute. The organisation of the Salvation Army was the work of Booth's eldest son, Bramwell. By the time Booth died in 1912 his Army had spread to 59 countries, and he numbered King Edward VII and many leading churchmen among his admirers.

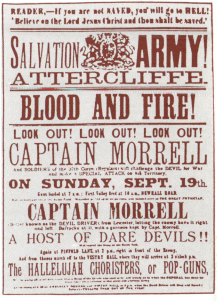

North of England poster for the Salvation Army

The badge of the Salvation Army

Public reaction to a Salvation Army procession

Elizabeth Garrett Anderson

A contemporary caricature

1836
Born 9th June in London
1860
Began studying medicine
1865
Passed examination of the Society of Apothecaries
1866
Opened dispensary for women in London
1871
Married James G. S. Anderson
1873
Member of the British Medical Association
1883-1903
Dean of London School of Medicine for Women
1908-1909
Britain's first woman mayor
1917
Died 17th December in Aldeburgh, Suffolk

Elizabeth Garrett Anderson was a pioneer feminist who became the first woman to qualify as a doctor in Britain - and through her work and example established the place of women in medicine.

Elizabeth Garrett was born in London in 1836. Her education at a school kept by two aunts of the poet Robert Browning, inspired her with ambitions for independence and the idea that women ought to be doctors.

Hospitals and universities all refused to give her training. She had to study privately. The only body that would admit her to its examinations was the Society of Apothecaries and she was licensed to practice in 1885 although the society later changed its rules to bar people who had not previously studied at a recognised medical school.

A year later she opened a dispensary for women in Marylebone, London, which was later converted into a hospital staffed by women (now known as the Elizabeth Garrett Anderson Hospital). In 1870 she took the degree of Doctor of Medicine at the Sorbonne in Paris.

In 1871 she married a shipowner, James George Skelton Anderson. They had two children, a son who followed his father as a shipowner, and a daughter who became a doctor.

Dr Anderson was the first - and for many years the only - woman elected to the British Medical Association. She lectured at the London School of Medicine for Women, founded in 1874, and was its dean for 20 years. In 1908-1909 she became the first woman mayor in Britain, as Mayor of Aldeburgh in Suffolk where she had her country home.

Elizabeth Garrett Anderson passing her exams before a French medical examination board

Elizabeth Garrett Anderson posing for a photograph

Dr. Barnardo

Thomas Barnardo was born in Dublin in 1845. He went to London to train as a doctor for missionary work in China. While still a medical student, however, he discovered that hundreds of poor children were sleeping rough every night. With the aid of Lord Shaftesbury and others he founded a mission in London's East End to feed and help these children, and abandoned his idea of going to China so that he could carry on with this work.

Barnardo opened his first home in Stepney, London, in September 1870. He provided shelter for 25 boys. Another lad, nicknamed 'Carrots', pleaded to come, too, but Barnardo knew he had money enough only for 25, and instead promised him the first vacancy. A few days later 'Carrots' was found dead of starvation. Barnardo vowed that whether he was in debt or not, he would never turn anyone away again. He put a large notice outside the home: *No destitute child is ever refused admittance.* It is still the motto of the Barnardo Homes.

Children 'found' by Dr Barnardo

Three years later Barnardo opened his first home for girls, at Barkingside in Essex. From the beginning he made sure his young charges were educated and given some training for adult life. Many children were sent as migrants to Canada, where he opened a home for them. By the time he died, worn out by his labours, Thomas Barnardo had admitted nearly 60,000 children to the 35 homes he had founded, and had given practical help to around 250,000 children.

1845
Born 4th July in Dublin
1866
Moved to London, began training as missionary
1868
Opened East End Juvenile Mission in Stepney
1870
Opened first Barnado home for boys in Stepney
1873
Married Syrie Elmslie; opened first home for girls
1879
Fellow of the Royal College of Surgeons, Edinburgh
1882
Began regular series of migrations to Canada
1889
Prevention of Cruelty to Children Act passed
1901
Naval training school for Barnardo's boys founded
1905
Died 19th September in Surbiton

An illustration from Dr Barnardo's publications showing the fate of a penniless child

Annie Besant

Annie Besant was one of the most controversial reformers. She fought to save mothers from having too many children, to help exploited workers, and for Indian independence, but her extreme enthusiasms and her religious views upset many people.

She was born in London in 1847, and made a disastrous marriage when she was 20 to Frank Besant, a schoolmaster who became a vicar. After six years as a battered wife Annie obtained a legal separation.

Mrs Besant now declared that she did not believe in God, and formed a close friendship with a fellow freethinker, Charles Bradlaugh, a politician. Her public speeches against Christianity brought abuse and violence from some of her listeners.

She had seen the suffering in families with too many children, and in 1877 she and Bradlaugh republished an old booklet by a doctor recommending that couples should practise birth control. They claimed that the public had the right to discuss social issues of this kind. They were prosecuted for obscene libel, but later acquitted on a legal technicality.

Mrs Besant then took a science degree at London University, became a Socialist and joined the Fabian Society. She organised a strike by badly-paid girls working in a match factory. Suddenly she adopted a new religion, Theosophy, and went to live in India, where she became involved in the early days of the struggle for Indian independence from British rule. She founded a Hindu college and the Home Rule for India League, and served as the President of the Indian National Congress for three years.

Sheet music cover for a humorous song ridiculing Bradlaugh and Besant's Atheism

An early photograph of Socialists *(below left)*

The strike committee of a 19th century union *(below)*

The badge of the Women's Social and Political Union

The Pankhursts

1858
Born 4th July in Manchester
1879
Married Richard Pankhurst
1880
Christabel Pankhurst born
1884
Joined Fabian Society
1898
Mr Pankhurst died
1903
Founded Women's Social and Political Union
1905
Began militant campaign; Christabel imprisoned
1908
Jailed for first time
1912
Jailed for conspiracy, went on hunger strike
1913
Freed and re-arrested 12 times under Cat and Mouse Act
1914
Visited United States and Russia
1919
Went to live in Canada
1926
Returned to England, joined Conservative Party
1928
Died 14th June in London, universal suffrage won

When Emmeline Goulden - better known by her married name of Pankhurst - was born in 1858, women were not allowed to vote. She was to lead the campaign for universal suffrage - votes for all adults.

Emmeline's parents introduced her to the idea of votes for women when she was a little girl. When she was 21 she married Richard Pankhurst, a successful lawyer and a campaigner for social reform. The two worked together to help the poor, until her husband died suddenly.

In 1903 Mrs Pankhurst and her three daughters, Christabel, Sylvia and Adela, and a few Socialist friends, started the Women's Social and Political Union, with the simple slogan: 'Votes for Women!' The Union first attracted attention when Christabel Pankhurst was imprisoned after disrupting a Liberal Party meeting.

Male politicians treated the whole thing as a joke, and the Suffragettes, as the campaigners became known, decided on more militant action. They interrupted public meetings, were arrested for causing a disturbance and fined, refused to pay and were jailed, time after time. Mrs Pankhurst organised demonstrations, mass meetings, protest marches, and appeals to MPs. When these tactics failed the Suffragettes smashed windows and chained themselves to railings. One threw herself in front of the king's horse at the Derby and was killed.

When the First World War broke out in 1914 the suffragettes suspended the fight for votes and worked hard to help the war effort. Women over 30 were given the vote in 1918. Universal suffrage became law on the day Emmeline Pankhurst died.

Emmeline Pankhurst and her daughter Christabel in prison uniform *(left)*

Emmeline Pankhurst's arrest *(below)*

Emmeline Pankhurst addressing crowds *(above)*

Christabel Pankhurst speaking in Trafalgar Square *(left)*

Lord Beveridge

World War Two soldier drinking to a 'Brave New World'

1879
Born 5th March in Rangpur, Bengal
1903
Sub-warden, Toynbee Hall
1905
Leader writer on the *Morning Post*
1908-1911
Set up labour exchanges and national insurance
1919
Made Knight Commander of the Order of the Bath
1919-1937
Director of the London School of Economics
1937-1944
Master of University College, Oxford
1942
Issued Beveridge Report ; married Janet Mair
1944-1945
Liberal MP
1946
Created Baron Beveridge
1963
Died 16th March in Oxford

When William Beveridge was at Oxford, the Master of Balliol suggested that he should try to 'discover why, with so much wealth in Britain, there continues to be so much poverty.' He set out to do just that.

Beveridge was born in India, where his father was serving in the Civil Service, but was educated in England. His first job was as sub-warden at Toynbee Hall, a charitable settlement in London's East End, and later became a leader-writer on the *Morning Post,* a newspaper of the day. In 1908 Winston Churchill, then President of the Board of Trade, asked him to join his staff. There Beveridge helped to set up the first labour exchanges and the first national insurance scheme.

During World War I Beveridge rose rapidly in the Civil Service, and was awarded a KCB. He left to become Director of the London School of Economics, and from there became Master of University College, Oxford. In World War II he was recalled to government service, but instead of the senior post he expected was put in charge of a committee on social insurance and allied services. This turned out to be the most important work of his life.

In 1942 the committee produced a report -popularly known as the Beveridge Report - which became the basis of the present-day Welfare State. Beveridge's plan proposed that everyone should be insured against unemployment, illness and old age, and that there should be a free health service.

He took no part in the setting up of the Welfare State he had envisaged. As he said: 'I have spent most of my life most happily in making plans for others to carry out.'

1942 newspaper announcement of the Beveridge Report

Beveridge tells how to
BANISH WANT

Cradle to grave plan | All pay— all benefit

SIR WILLIAM BEVERIDGE'S Report, aimed at abolishing Want in Britain, is published today.

He calls his Plan for Social Security a revolution under which "every citizen willing to serve according to his powers has at all times an income sufficient to meet his responsibilities."

Here are his chief proposals:

All social insurance—unemployment, health, pension — lumped into one weekly contribution for all citi— income limit—from duke to dustman.

These payments, in the case of employ

Men 4s. 3d.   Employer 3s. 3d.
Women 3s. 6d.   Employer 2s. 6d.

Cradle to the grave benefits for al' including:

Free medical, dental, eyesight and hospital treatment;

Children's allowances of 8s. a week each, after the first child.

Increases in unemployment benefit (40s. for a couple) and abolition of the means test; industrial pension in place of workmen's compensation.

A charter for housewives, including marriage grant up to £10; maternity grant of £4 (and 36s. for 13 weeks for a paid worker); widow's benefit; separation and divorce provision; free domestic help in time of sickness.

Old age pensions rising to 40s. for a married couple on retirement.

Funeral grants up to £20.

To work the scheme a new Ministry of Social Security would open Security

Sir Allen Lane

More than anyone else, the publisher Allen Lane was responsible for making good books cheap enough for most people to afford. He accomplished this by starting the paperback series Penguin Books.

He was born in Bristol in 1902, the son of an architect, and named Allen Lane Williams. When he was 16 he was invited to join the Bodley Head, a publishing firm started by John Lane, a relative of his mother. Lane had no children, and wanted someone to carry on the business and his name. So young Allen changed his name to Allen Lane and settled down to learn the publishing business.

In the 1930s the Bodley Head was in financial trouble, and Allen Lane, by then chairman, thought it might be saved by producing a series of cheap paperback reprints. His fellow directors were not convinced, so Lane went ahead at his own expense.

The inexpensive and portable nature of Penguins made them widely popular during long periods of waiting for members of the armed forces in World War II

He published the first 10 Penguin titles in 1935. He priced them at 6d (2p) each. Booksellers and publishers predicted disaster, but Woolworth's decided to stock Penguins and after a shaky start the books started to sell briskly. Soon afterwards Lane left the Bodley Head.

He began commissioning new books and also fought for the right of publishers to issue important books without censorship. In 1960 he issued D. H. Lawrence's *Lady Chatterley's Lover*, which was thought to be obscene and to have a corrupting influence. He was prosecuted but won after a sensational court case which changed the legal view of what is fit to be published.

Lane was knighted for his services to publishing and shortly before his death was made a Companion of Honour, a rare distinction.

1902
Born 21st September in Bristol
1919
Joined the Bodley Head and changed his name
1925
Became a director
1930
Became chairman
1935
Issued first 10 Penguins
1936
Left the Bodley Head
1941
Married Lettice Lucy Orr
1946
First Penguin Classic, *The Odyssey*, published
1952
Received knighthood
1960
Won *Lady Chatterley's Lover* court case
1969
Made Companion of Honour
1970
Died 7th July in Northwood, near London

Evening Standard

42.421   WEDNESDAY, NOVEMBER 2, 1960   ●● 2½d.

Jury reach historic decision after 3 hours

THE INNOCENCE OF LADY CHATTERLEY

She's cleared after 6-day trial

APPLAUSE AT OLD BAILEY

Evening Standard Reporter

'Lady' Chatterley's Lover is NOT obscene. So the jury at the Old Bailey decided this afternoon after being out for three hours.

There was loud clapping and applause from the back of the court when the foreman of the jury announced the verdict. Ushers cried loudly: "Silence — silence." The clapping and applause stopped.

...with their plans to issue D. H. Lawrence's novel as a 3s. 6d. paperback.

Mr. Gerald Gardiner, QC, who had led the defence, asked for the prosecution to contribute a substantial amount towards the cost of the case. The judge refused.

Mr. Gardiner said the prosecution had been brought as a test case. It had been a decision of the Director of Public Prosecutions to obtain a decision under the new Obscene Publications Act and to see how it works.

The American case'

Mr. Gardiner said that all the questions concerned in the case were considered "in the American case" and then it was stated that the publication of the book was not contrary to the public interest.

The costs of the six-day trial had been "very...

'NOW WE CAN GO AHEAD' SAYS PENGUIN CHIEF

Evening Standard Reporter

Sir Allen Lane, head of Penguin Books, ran from the Old Bailey this afternoon after the Lady Chatterley verdict to meet a barrage of waving hands outstretched in congratulation. "I feel marvellous," he said, smiling and breathless.

Exultantly he told me: "Now we can go ahead with distributing the novel. But it will be 10 days before it is in general circulation."

The 200,000 copies we had printed at a cost of more than £18,000 had been sent to book shops throughout the provinces for a publication date last August.

They had not reached booksellers at the time it was launched after the prosecution was launched.

Fair

"The trade was very fair and every copy we could trace came back again; from a few which went on sale accidentally in Nottingham.

"The shops that had reached were in Scotland, Northern Ireland and Northern England.

"How many copies will we print in addition to the 200,000 now that the book has been cleared? I should think we could do with a new paper printing press.

"We have fought the case and published the book because we felt it was right and proper to publish Lawrence's work as a whole.

"It is a big landmark in the...

Press cutting after the court case over the novel *Lady Chatterley's Lover*

Dame Cicely Saunders

1918
Born 22nd June in London
1940
Left university to train as a nurse
1944
Qualified as a state registered nurse
1945
Awarded BA degree, with Diploma in Social and Public Administration
1947
Qualified as an almoner
1957
Qualified as a doctor
1958
Started research on control of pain in terminal illness
1967
St Christopher's opened; awarded OBE
1974
Became Fellow of Royal College of Physicians
1980
Created DBE; married Professor Marian Bohusz
1981
Awarded £90,000 Templeton Prize for Progress in Religion

One of the greatest reforms of modern times has been the establishment of hospices where people who are terminally ill can end their lives in comfort. The hospice movement owes its existence to one determined woman, Cicely Saunders.

Cicely Mary Strode Saunders came from a wealthy London family. She went to Oxford University, but when World War II broke out left her studies to train as a nurse. During her three-year training she developed severe back trouble, and though she qualified she was told she must give up nursing.

She went back to Oxford, completed her degree, and then trained as a hospital almoner (medical social worker). She had become a devout Christian.

During her work as an almoner she became friends with a dying Polish patient, David Tasma. They discussed the idea of hospices, and when Tasma died he left Cicely Saunders £500 'to be a window in your home'. It took her 19 years to build the home around the window. She realised that to run the kind of hospice she planned she would need to be a doctor. So she returned to her studies and qualified for her third career at the age of 38. At once she began research on the control of pain for people dying of such illnesses as cancer.

It took her a further nine years to raise the money to open St Christopher's Hospice in Sydenham, South London. It was the first research and teaching hospice, dedicated to the control of pain. Cicely Saunders received a OBE for her work the same year. In 1980 she was created a Dame Commander of the British

Dame Cicely Saunders chatting to a patient

Empire, and married Professor Marian Bohusz, a Polish artist.

By the late 1980s there were more than a hundred hospices for the terminally ill in Britain where, as Dame Cicely put it, patients can 'close the book neatly', free of pain.

The legal process of reform

Mr. Pitt, the Prime Minister, addressing the House of Commons in 1793

The parliamentary process of reform

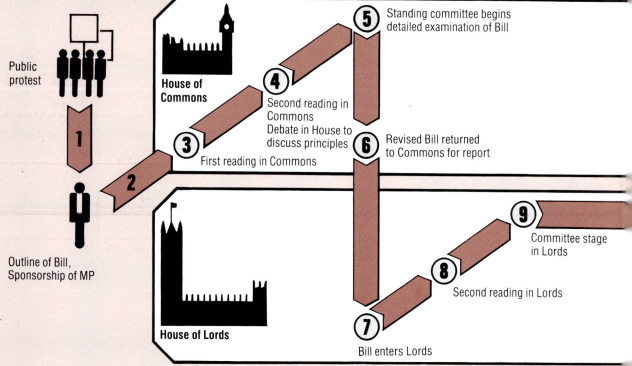

Public protest

1

Outline of Bill, Sponsorship of MP

2

House of Commons

3
First reading in Commons

4
Second reading in Commons
Debate in House to discuss principles

5 Standing committee begins detailed examination of Bill

6 Revised Bill returned to Commons for report

House of Lords

7
Bill enters Lords

8
Second reading in Lords

9
Committee stage in Lords

Some recent Acts of Parliament

Rating (Dis...)
Act...

1978 CHA...

An Act to amend the law r...
in respect of premises used...
invalids; and for purposes...

B E IT ENACTED by the Queen's mo...
with the advice and consent...
Temporal, and Commons, i...
assembled, and by the authority of th...

Provisions for England...

1.—(1) Subject to the provisions of th...
rity for any area in England and Wa...
in respect of the rates chargeable on a...
is situated in the area and to which this...

(2) This section applies to—

Employment Protecti...
(Consolidation) Act 1...

1978 CHAPTER 44

An Act to consolidate certain enactments
rights of employees arising out of their e...
and certain enactments relating to the i...
employers; to industrial tribunals; to reco...
certain benefits; to conciliation officers...
certain benefits; to conciliation officers... [31st
Employment Appeal Tribunal.

B E IT ENACTED by the Queen's most Excellent M...
with the advice and consent of the Lords...
Temporal, and Commons, in this prese...
assembled, and by the authority of the same, as fol...

PART I

PARTICULARS OF TERMS OF EMPLOYM...

Written particulars of terms of employ...

1.—(1) Not later than thirteen weeks after th...
an employee's period of employment with an...
employer shall give to the employee a writte...
accordance with the following provisions of this...

(2) An employer shall in a statement under th...
(a) identify the parties;
(b) specify the date when the employment b...
(c) state whether any employment with a p...
counts as part of the employee's cont...
employment, and, if so, specify the...
continuous period of employment beg...

(3) A statement under this section shall cont...
particulars of the terms of employment as a...

Rent Act 1977

1977 CHAPTER 42

An Act to consolidate the Rent Act 1968, Parts III, IV
and VIII of the Housing Finan... ... 1972, the Rent
Act 1974, sections 7 to 10 of th...
Subsidies Act 1975, and certa...
with amendments to give effec...
of the Law Commission.

B E IT ENACTED by the Queen's mo...
with the advice and consent...
Temporal, and Commons,...
assembled, and by the authority of t...

PART...

PRELIMI...

Protected and stat...

1. Subject to this Part of this...
dwelling-house (which may be s...
let as a separate dwelling is...
purposes of this Act.

Any reference in this Act...
construed accordingly.

2.—(1) Subject to this Part o...
(a) after the terminatio...
dwelling-house the p...
termination, was the...
house shall, if and s...
... his reside...

Post Office Act 1977

1977 CHAPTER 44

An Act to increase the maximum number of members
of the Post Office. [29th July 1977]

B E IT ENACTED by the Queen's most Excellent Majesty, by and
with the advice and consent of the Lords Spiritual and
Temporal, and Commons, in this present Parliament
assembled, and by the authority of the same, as follows:—

1.—(1) The word "nineteen" shall be substituted for the *Membership*
word "twelve" in section 6(2) of the Post Office Act 1969 *of the Post*
(composition of the Post Office). *Office.*
... of section 6(2) of the Post Office Act 1969 *1969 c. 48.*

Community Service
Offenders (Scotland) Ac...

1978 CHAPTER 49

An Act to make provision as respects the perfor...
unpaid work by persons convicted or p...
probation in Scotland; and for connected pu... [31st J...

B E IT ENACTED by the Queen's most Excellent Majest...
with the advice and consent of the Lords Spi...
Temporal, and Commons, in this present P...
assembled, and by the authority of the same, as follows:—

1.—(1) Subject to the provisions of this Act, where a person
of or over 16 years of age is convicted of an offence punishable
... other than an offence the sentence fo... which
... of dealing with him in...

**Returned to Commons
for approval of
Lords amendments**

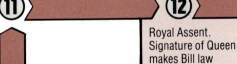

Law enacted

(11) ──── (12) ────

**Royal Assent.
Signature of Queen
makes Bill law**

(10)

**Report stage
in Lords**

National Health Service
Act 1977

1977 CHAPTER 49

An Act to consolidate certain provisions relating to the
health service for England and Wales; and to repeal
certain enactments relating to the health service which
have ceased to have any effect. [29th July 1977]

B E IT ENACTED by the Queen's most Excellent Majesty, by and
with the advice and consent of the Lords Spiritual and
Temporal, and Commons, in this present Parliament
assembled, and by the authority of the same, as follows:—

PART I

SERVICES AND ADMINISTRATION

Functions of the Secretary of State

1.—(1) It is the Secretary of State's duty to continue the *Secretary*
promotion in England and Wales of a comprehensive health *of State's*
service designed to secure improvement— *duty as to*
(a) in the physical and mental health of the people of those *health service.*
countries, and
(b) in the prevention, diagnosis and treatment of illness,
and for that purpose to provide or secure the effective provision
of services in accordance with this Act.

(2) The services so provided shall be free of charge except
in so far as the making and recovery of charges is expressly
provided for by or under any enactment, whenever passed.

Milestones of social history

1750

1795 Speenhamland System of Poor Relief
1708 Thomas Malthus – Essay on Population
1799/1800 Combination Acts (T.U.s illegal)

1800

1801 First census
1824 Combination Acts repealed
1825 First locomotive railway line – Stockton-Darlington
1829 Metropolitan Police founded
1831/1832 Cholera epidemic
1832 First Reform Act (upper middle class franchise)
1833 Abolition of slavery in British Empire
1833 First effective Factory Act
1834 New Poor Law (workhouse system – nationwide)
1834 Women given vote in municipal elections
1834 Grand National Consolidated Trades Union and Tolpuddle Martyrs
1836 Registration of births, deaths and marriages
1839 Rowland Hill's penny post
1839 People's Charter first presented to parliament
1842 Mines Act
1844 Railway Passengers' Act
1847 Ten Hour Factory Act
1848 First Public Health Act

1850

1867 Second Reform Act (urban, mass, working class, propertied franchise)
1868 First T.U.C.
1870 Forster's Education Act
1872 Second Ballot
1875 Artisans Dwellings Act (permitting slum clearance)
1876 Attendance at school made compulsory
1884 Third Reform Act (rural, working class, propertied franchise)
1889 Dockers' Strike
1890 Free education for all
1892 First Labour M.P. Kier Hardie
1893 Independent Labour Party founded

1900

1903	Women's Social and Political Union
1903	School Meals Act
1908	Old Age Pensions Act
1909	First suffragette on hunger strike
1909	People's Budget
1911	Parliament Act (payment of M.P.s and abolition of Lords' veto)
1911	National Insurance Act
1913	Cat and Mouse Act
1914/1918	First World War
1918	Manhood suffrage at 21: female suffrage at 30
1919	First woman M.P. Lady Astor
1919	First council houses
1919	Sex Disqualification Act
1926	General Strike
1929	End of workhouse system
1929	Wall Street Crash
1930	Beginning of Great Depression
1934	Unemployment Act
1936	Jarrow Hunger March
1939/1945	Second World War
1942	Beveridge Report
1944	Butler's Education Act
1945	Family Allowances Act
1946	National Insurance Act
1946	National Health Service Act
1946	New Towns Act
1946/1947	Nationalisation of coal, civil airlines, canals, railways, road haulage
1949	Nationalisation of iron and steel

THE DAWN OF HOPE.

Mr. LLOYD GEORGE'S National Health Insurance Bill provides for the insurance of the Worker in case of Sickness.

Support the Liberal Government
in their policy of
SOCIAL REFORM.

1950

1951	G.C.E. introduced
1958	C.S.E. introduced
1959	First comprehensive schools
1961	Immigration Act
1965	Abolition of death penalty
1965	Race Relations Board set up
1967	Abortion Act
1969	Universal suffrage at 18
1970	Equal Pay Act
1973	Britain joins E.E.C.
1973	World Oil Crisis
1975	Sex Discrimination Act
1976	Race Relations Act
1980	Housing Act
1981	First race riots (Southall, Toxteth and St. Paul's)
1983	People's March for Jobs
1984–1985	Miners' Strike
1986	Abolition of the metropolitan councils (G.L.C. etc.)

Useful addresses

The Labour Party Young Socialists
150 Walworth Road
London
SE17 1JT

The Young Communists League
16 St Johns Street
London
EC1M 4AL

The Conservative Central Office
32 Smith Square
London
SW1

The National League of Young Liberals
1 Whitehall Place
London
SW1

Community Service Volunteers (CSV)
237 Pentonville Road
London
N1

Voluntary Services Overseas (VSO)
9 Belgrave Square
London
SW1

Careers and Occupational Information Centre
Manpower Services Commission
Moorfoot
Sheffield
S1 4PQ

Nursing and Hospital Careers Centre
121–123 Edgeware Road
London
W2 2HX

Index

SCIENTISTS

EXPLORERS

BACON	BOYLE	NEWTON
HALLEY	THE HERSCHELS	JENNER
DALTON	FARADAY	DARWIN
KELVIN	LISTER	MAXWELL
THOMSON	FLEMING	CRICK

FROBISHER	HUDSON	COOK
PARK	FRANKLIN	STURT
ROSS	LIVINGSTONE	SPEKE
STANLEY	YOUNGHUSBAND	SCOTT
SHACKLETON	FUCHS	FIENNES